Caviar

Sarah Fletcher

Out-Spoken Press
London

Published by Out-Spoken Press,
Unit 39, Containerville
1 Emma Street
London, E2 9FP

A CIP record for this title is available from the British Library.

First edition published 2022
ISBN: 978-1-8384272-4-5

Typeset in Adobe Caslon
Design by Patricia Ferguson
Printed and bound by Print Resources

Out-Spoken Press is supported using public funding by the National
Lottery through Arts Council England and a grant from the Inclusive
Indies Fund administered by Spread the Word.

Supported using public funding by

**ARTS COUNCIL
ENGLAND**

'My fur coat's sold, oh, Lord ain't it cold
But I'm not gonna holler, 'cause I've still got a dollar
And when I get low
Oh, I get high'

— Marion Sunshine, as performed by Ella Fitzgerald

Contents

The Bed Is Not a Window, The Bed Is a Two-Way Mirror

Have we met?
Has sleep, its arguments, ornaments, glyphs,
too brought you here... to wink with me
before we put back our bodies?

Sleep... is jungled by these licks
of tentacles. Sleep
is dragged by bad dreams' jellyfish. Perhaps
we met. Perhaps you glimpsed a personality.

The poet to the reader: you don't know me!
The reader to the poet, painstakingly, repeats
you do not know me! *Is it affirmation, argument, echo?*
This is no relationship! This is escape artistry!

Blowjob

I have been to the weighing
Of souls. I have ridden the velvet
Black horizon of American
Highways, shuttling
A Catholic priest
Towards bellies of stars.

I have seen the planets
Puree into streamers
From the drink
And from the
Speed.

An act of service,
An assessment,
Or even therapy.
Violated eyes that become
Clean with your looking.
Host of the divine bistro!
Actor-doctor with the will
To tease the lamb to Easter dinner!
Sing the newborn from a cave!
What did you expect, a rose?

A Slap In The Face… of Nature

Heat
Bends through the 'party room'
Like a tropical snake. Our drinking amps
The creature's red, systolic turnings.
We are arriving to night's final station.
C'mon babies. Time to ride.

A man in a black bear suit sees a woman in a brown bear suit.

Second thought. He doesn't see her. He has followed her.

Through summer's fluffy mists, he smelt

Her daybed, sussed the perimeter of her desire.

He'd known of her urine for years. A perfect match.

He zips his fluffy suit, and enters through her window.

Swans drinking white wine
Are just called swines.
He is
Explaining the subtraction
Between event and labour value.
Operette. Acropolis. Fawns fawning.

So bored, I tend the moon's aquarium.
Tears turn to teeth of serpents
When they reach the water. Now there are lots of snakes.

They arch their delicious heads for breath.
They want to slither back to my eye's worm-womb,
O linger Sapphos of the lash-line! Please don't leave!
He grabs a girl one by the neck and bites its head.

I'll give you details if you want. He was so slang.
He was circus.
He
Bodied me his body.

'Why do forty year old narcissistic cokeheads
Always want to slap me in the face?'

It feels overly specific and obscene
To include a pronoun. It pours a drink. It pours
Me
A drink.
I drink it.

I'd rather be
Summoning angels.
Not angels but halos.
Not halos but the idea of halos.
The idea of a woman,
Dreaming of halos.

When he slapped me in the face
He was Francis of Assisi
Preaching to a bird.
Francis of Assisi
Blessing a bunny.
He put his fat thumb in a hole in my tights
And pulled. Ladders like lightning up my thigh:

Francis of Assisi
Causing thunder.

He is slurring something something partner while
Someone is in Dalston saying something
Something husband. How does she dress?

I take comfort in the deaths of species.
Plants. Gone. Yes. All the plants.
Nervous systems no longer so nervous.
He changes the music to my favourite song.
C'mon baby, time to ride.

I am digitally reincarnated into the past;
Born backe as Baudelaire's petty whores.
All of them. Yes. All the whores.

Washing at the End of the Night, Which is the Next Day's Afternoon

A foot, my own, can be either
collaborator or accessory to a cause,
especially when looming its sole
across the surface of a bath to gauge the heat.

A woman's foot, when shed from fishnet tights, is a free fish,
a small gesticulator, circling toes to ripple.
This is foreplay for the end of progress…
Hush now; it is entering the whirlpool,

which sucks us to a refracted world.
Enter a garden, where the air writes it all down.
Nymphs, washing; sororal twins
to stiff Greek columns. Gowns as melting candles.

Exhausting to find the universal in this caper.
Psychic hygiene in a restored Venetian arch.
Temperate is perfect. Water, perfect.
I am empty. I have killed my mother in myself.

Beginning Again, Without a Title

Or, it was like that field trip in Madrid
(I helped the kids board the autobús
while their tanned dads hid hard-ons
like magician's doves)…when you entered my museum
of sneaking looks,
entered like a deck of cards
hidden beneath the garish sleaze
of the sleeviest Spanish guitarist.

Behind glass, the lingering gaze.
Behind more glass, hands holding.

You say of course that you prefer red wine.
Well that's boring. Let's change the scene.

I told him that he has a sleazy face.
He didn't even know who Serge Gainsbourg was,
which I tucked into my accumulating hatreds:
a useful tool for later,
like a plastic knife in an asylum.

I am thinking of a mother, my own. She said
I'd make myself dizzy
With my epigenetic love for fizz…

that familial tolerance towards blurriness,
whether photographs or pharmaceuticals,
that abstract lusciousness of oblivion
so served in cups, or shots, or glasses.

People should feel more ashamed.

That slug voice of yours: does it not make you feel embarrassed?
You should tuck it somewhere, safely. I have a place in mind.
Or pour salt across the bastard entirely.
My kitchen's waiting, like a school girl, restless. Cupboards
scream.

The dolphins and even the seals know.
The spew of froth
calls out your name, like witches' arms,
which take on a new terror
when crawling from the water.
You're a bastard.

It isn't you, but the feelings I put on to you:
test-tubed and
plain as a noughties model.
The lapse between experiment and esperanto.

My joy's thinking of you the way a dog
may think of you. Then, I can like you.

This isn't the first time.
The gun is jumped and child crucified.
The gun's implied and child crucified.
Chekhov is dead. The child's long since died.
Sometimes I think: they're just like this.
They are always like this, please let me
be like this, so I can be like them. O look I am.

I find my hands holding my thigh the way I'd chide a child
for eating over hours, or like the neck
of that rapist swan set out by feminists.

She conjured neon fairy energy they said.

She could kill herself over it. Poor thing.
                         You'd be afraid to even cough.

By she, of course, O I mean I — but when
it's seen again the thought comes as a crab
dredged from the darkest pit of sea
— so boil me.

I cough my guilt in little rosaries;
they wetly love my cashmeres and my silks.

They curl like small snails into pearls
to hide from the dynamic of my shame.

Naming the butterfly beneath the impulse
taxidermies any feeling underneath.

Like chloroform, casual as sweaters,
is dressed on sins or even inaction…

there's still the rosary, each beaded name
adorned without being adored.

How do you send a stranger into sleep?
Here's another glass, a nightcap, maybe…

'No harm no fowl.'

His long white neck's strung like a line of coke
across a blackened Bible. He is against the sky

wings of cocaine sprawl as auras
from his slouching shoulders. He's the

fallen soldier falling from his fallen fathers.
A dustling on a book whose author I have killed.

And what of Leda. She combs her hair
on an Aberystwyth beach,
a pint in hand. The swan approaches
from the ocean, baring teeth.
She asks him for a fag, and he
presents his beak.

I pursue you like a diagnosis I do not believe in
but still am interested in the medication.

I don't know. Just sweat on me.
Sometimes things exist cerebrally.

Here is a liver. Here's my heart.
I serve them often, these days, with butter.

As long as you can swallow easily,
they go down like a treat.

The more you believe in pop lyrics
the closer you are to God.

My Second Vision of True Love at the Bank of a Bender

I meet you in the stairwell clutch-

    ing my little almanac

        of trembling things

    leaving my mouth   honey

*

Metaphor, be gone. It really
was. I despair
the parallel line of logic
        (pull my braid).

There *was* a swan, crying diamonds
in the corner, beak fluffy
with white wine and the excruciating hatred
of its secrets.

There *were* the house mice, being juggled by
boy-virgins and I felt
that pink, diaphanous bomb
shake the pillars of your boots.

*

Then
there was your thigh snaking mine
in that light room in Clapton   we were
drunk the light

was
filtered through colours of ocean   our bodies
switched   flipping from fish to man
all night   ugliest phosphorous, lit

Darling you are the template I dream
Of pouring my lips unto

Batter to mould before baking

Here I am with the decision of Dogs:
Come   Stay   Christ

*

'Unengulfable desire precluding touch', or, consider:

the inside of your mouth: part

stadium lights, part
praying mantis: consider your eyes,
wrong axes, sinking towards different
symphonies: consider, mouth, part me

*

dream of ten thousand guinea pigs peek-
ing heads through the waves' troughs
such softness   such wet

*

That night was like floating but
in reverse

thinking of you between
icicles and monkey bars

each lip bringing the neon-blue
lacework of wings

towards the pressed butterfly of this
elite vacation.

I pour resin over the pirated moment.
I return it to sender,

make a paperweight. There.
There. Perfect.

I (seeping with preclusive love) shall give this creature to
the Cairenes air in which you live,

before we wake to re-fall out of touch

God dammit.

To You With A Guitar

after Sean Shibe's rendition of LAD by Julia Wolfe

Guitar uncrinkling any sound: the cough,
the rough of papers in that lady's bag
as she shifts to cross her legs.

Of course,
I worry
about the hazards

of breathing in so much
noise. What can you do but hope
that it will scrape you clean?

Let it in,
a rod threaded with cloth,
jabbing up a flute's nose.

To another poet, even you,
living inside this sterile throb could be
like living under God; God,
I agree; I
want it to last forever —

The future mistakes and yawns:
A word.
A woman hit. A nuclear bomb.
The messenger will suffer well, make no mistake:
I am checking in.

You have ghostwritten this poem from ten years in the future
and you have ruined my life.

Country Matters

DEDICATION

Flamingo, urchin, bestiaric beast:
Paroling city matters, you reform
From pigeon's dirty feather to a quill.

A parlour game: we reach the dovetailing
Between those singing spasmic pities that
We summon, and the dank urbanity

You wreak. It comes to punish this reserve.
Love: whether zoo, circus, menagerie,
All matters of a name more so than form,

Let us rush towards autowilderness,
Strifed with wet, chaotic humours.
Erotic prescience : I sense us : one.

We've taken flyte, so let us rest in shelter,
Into the original of the world,
Nothing can stop our loved country from mattering.

ONE

*

There is a woman turning a woman turning
itself on

Sick hydra starting up   I dream
of sea becoming seaworthy to sea

The sea drownsy   in its offensive capability

Drownsy Baby   thirsting in its sleep   *Hush now*

Totemic fetish or mnemonic logo :   her offensive cheep :
untid'ly starting up for the tide :   *cheap*

*

You cannot scry in your own silver when
its ripples split the vision

They cannot peer into a depth they've mined   and filled

Selfsang in their own gags   Dull drams overfilled

                            -spilling unward

Eat your eyesight, bastard   *Ring yourself unfit*

*

Q: Where has this water gone? Why disappear?

A: Add an arch to the middle of valour. There's your answer.

In the mean time, build a city   Then build a countryside
for balance

*

Now, not sea at all   They become

ardor's coldened shoulder   Ardor eccentric
Radiating inward

Throttling at different purposes and speeds.

*

TWO

An altared state urned in a loss of verse
Severed then served with coming of the morning
My love has earned this insurrective swerve
That seeks to crash the calming of his mourning

*

You rest inequality

If I was embedded in a painscape, it'd be different

Q: Where do you rest?
A: Camped out
in the bedazzled house
of his runtish fantasy

His House Believes …

As it is now, there is
an asterisk to every kiss

*

Let me rest
in that nest of those pink, electric branches

There, there is safety

*

THREE

*

To have a handle on something is to have the capacity to turn
it on or off

*

What I cuse him of I cuse myself

*

When they are together, their shape
is endless and content

The sea drinking the sea   The sea is drinking
                                                             the sea

*

The vulvic octopus dies with her young
Meanwhile, I: waste   with my   youth

The staggering dear does not accept my hand,
fawning and shrill. Cast off from my ilk, my hart.

*

FOUR

*

The dysgenic body's calling back to you,
Consumed and mated. Her dysphoric flesh.
Both locked within this sick twin study;
She'll do anything, at last, to prove you're bad.

*

As gravity holds each wave in vassalage.
As without gods, there is none mastered;
O gypsum child: I see through your age,
Such wind wrinkles water alabastered.

*

Fair Access faring more than anything
     I wish them want : I wish them will : I wish

When I clang against the ground
In my metal shoes   I am no one's home
I am outside for the first time in sixteen weeks

I am a piece of change in this purse of the rain
That swallows the world and brushes
My skin like the whitest of white mink coats

———O⊸———

I always knew when they expanded.
They grew each time there was my own
Return-to-form, which came as a stricken
Return to carnality. Boréd, Boréd.
Returning to the so-called civility of
The dirty deflated red balloon.

Where my love enacts The Good Fight :
Wrestling the ars antiqua from the mouths
Of the princess, and the prince, and the dog.
The rain outside falls in long streams, like serpents
Returning to carnality. Boréd, Boréd.
Following their pink yawns into the dirt   *When will the rain…?*

INTERROGATION IN THE PALACE OF BACKWARDS:

What is the colour of the man you left here?.

—Moth

What is the name of his mother, of his father?.

—The upward scream of a cicada, the sky

Purple beaded necklaces racing

Why do you come here? What do you seek?

—The air inside had told me it was itchy.

It had been untouched for years.

It told me just my breath would satisfy its itch.

That all I had to do was step inside.

Why are you covered in algae
When you should be covered
In honey? He asked me this as
I removed my clothes. But I came
To this place as one of Redon's swamp flowers,
I knew I was going to stay a swamp flower.
I just needed his pale knuckles
To light the candle in my lantern
In my head. I asked him to do this,
Green and wet.
I asked him very, very nicely.

And my hearing, as touch seems
To be the only rule in this Palace
Where my wound is always
More eloquent than my mouth.

It wails. It hurts. but still
It bites. It is biting over and over
And over and over
Again. Please, Daddy. Just one more time.

○

When I arrived, his room was filled
With petty atmospherics. Lodestone
And amber. Ten perverse spangles.
Albino peacock feathers
À la Akhmatova. He poured
The wine, which had been waiting, perhaps
For many hours. It uncoiled slowly in the unfit glass.
He was cradled in his bacchanalia; I came along as
He staggered to quench the cusp of his desire

The stellectric welkin sobs
With lightning.
Thunder sobs. Rain doesn't sob and hides,
Tucked in the cloud. Please fall.
It arrives in colours instead of streams:
Purple beaded necklaces racing
To the ground, punctuated by
The forks of white that never reach the ground.

○

It starts like a dream-in-waiting
And that dream is a docked
Oil tanker on a banks of a desert.
That dream is a supine skyscraper of rust
Waiting for a signal
To jettison.
I stand on the banks. The waves
Are rough, like gravel shovelling itself
Into my palm. A firework goes off:
Its ashy tendrils meeting their watery reflection
In the Horizon, the meeting place of
My self and my Sake.
I look back into the desert and see I have arrived.

At the Palace of Backwards
I am unable to tell whether Crisis
Is a participant or observer.
Regardless I am told I must enter the Palace

It was September 2016 when he decided to ring
A belle-de-nuit, which was a hilarious idea
Until she arrived slicked in black and
He disapproved   *You are an itchy*
Little trigger aren't you? He snarled
The taffeta was ridiculous
And made me rumble for an enormous
Amount of icing sugar.
This was a desire which was never
Completed. The sound of the evening
With its indiscernible location
Stuck in my mind with its constant, pink yawning.
He told me to shut up and make myself a milkshake.
He said that it would help me fall asleep

Cruelty was fed at my teat
Like a ball of static. Its borders
Were always in negotiation
But

When will the rain come back from the water?

It was the year vanilla became more
Expensive than silver

Dogsbodies were scattered outside
On every corner, busying themselves…

I was leaving the car of a stranger when
Some one asked me
When will the rain come back from the water?

I opened my mouth and in
one simultaneous voice   occurred:

——————O∘——————

Looking at the sun, straight,
So that its imprint stains into my eyelids
When I stir away, I feel the beatitude
Of addicts and their gaped mouths. Or
Just one addict, whose mouth I knew so well,
The moment before he
Fell asleep in a bed
Which was my bed, which I was in,
And this happened every night.

In the Palace of Backwards, my name is Lunamastix
Because they fear I am a sleeper agent.
They bring me to dinner in a red velvet gown.
Goddress flamingo. Wine in my mouth feels
Like feathers. We start with dessert
Which is pink rose petals
And finish with gruel, which I paint
Extravagantly all over my mouth.

Sound comes dressed in drag.
The record says it is folk violin but I know it is
A coyote with a jagged tooth
That wails with pain each time
It bites the roadkilled deer,

Some days I awake to find the palace
Has become a re-education camp.
I am far away from the banks where I waited
For the oil tanker to slip into the horizon.
I wonder if I am losing my sight

24

Caviar

Beginning again
At the apple's technology,
like a ninth irradiated life,
I eat the juicy fruit — a top-shelf, porno-picnic moment,
glittering like the piss of a baby rabbit —
to see its inner workings. Bam. Enter. Swiftly: thought.

> (In the back garden, birds start chanting:
> We're lifting from mechanic sleep!)

In turn, I chant: fuck.
I am handed the plot; I add an I.
Pilot! Pilot! Lift off. Here we go.
The apple's algorithm penetrates.
We fly: zoom, zoom.

Hard-drive, girl-child, rainbow-fish....
Consumable tidbits from my dream's wet market.
It all unspirals from my apple-woman mind, the virus,
more impressive than first man, or angel, or circuit.

I feel the fault deliciously,
Straining its sensuous motions to the face of God,

fireworking the filthiest collection, moving alively.
I unsat the drasticated chair the world forgot.

At first the world was fruitful:
        wilful mass theories shooting.
So goes the exponential ticking
        of hateful, playful evolution.

'Life is':
waking
as if moving underwater,
from the only dream
that anybody dreams:
of promiscuity
with dignity, yes, waking slowly,
awash with sweat
on the upstairs couch
of a stranger's party,
rolled in white flannel
and surrounded by empty
baggies and bottles, we are
disgusting little beasts, and moreover
sent into this abattoir
so hungry…

> (Interruption: Love Poem.
> I am in Whitstable. Clouds? Used tissues,
> scarred by needles of planes.
> Beach? Empty, awash with footsteps all the same.
> My oyster-mind can connect trifling things in loose
> systems; no
>   centre.
> You? Beneath the sun's radical surgery, strange-holding
> your face, I see you, smiling.
> We kiss deeply (though the shapes of kisses now escape
> my mind,
> **like** imagining a country one's never seen… oh my
> love…
> my darling… we have no idea what's coming…))

I'm ill for weeks. Each dirty image exhausted,
each surface sweat, bones bored with pain,
I take to the spheres. Namely,
that anonymous yellow man
on Google Maps. I drag him to and fro,
to exorcise power over fiefdoms I'll never touch.

I settle on an oil rig, at sea, Caspian sea…
Bulimic waves throw up jetsam's scattered cards.

                    (Birds are chanting: dive! dive! dive!)

So I dive! I am
being haunted by God. Spores of faith
find my every populace. Stunning plankton
filtering stained glass. I break the black
and the hermetic. Sturgeon-angels,
whose skeletons complete their hi-tech weapons,
triage me into arms. Love.

God reads my mind zoonotically, a thought
so gorgeous I cannot bring myself to choose it.

I climb the velvet lime scaffold even deeper,
colours razed with mounting pleasure… I find

God's opera: Real Love. Willing the sturgeons,
those guardians of Eden, living fossils, to sing
lingering, chamber music.

How they lap in sorrow's playpen,
their organs knitting together.
And inside those sturgeons
hundreds of eggs: glistened and statutory prayers,

which express exactly what one wants
in the correct language, the first time precisely,
to the correct grant-body…
the only dream that anybody dreams.

I mourn the eggs…
darling abducted princesses,
quivers-in-waiting,
packed by the damnéd caravan
into those coils, clean and saved.

> And most beautiful and sad of all
> is how those sturgeons give them up,
> even offer their white stomachs to the surface,
> not from stupidity but hope,
> to poachers with their boorish
> fishnets,
> who attack this wet, rejected heaven,
> traffic it to oligarchic plates
> It is entirely my fault…but if the men arrive
> I say, amen, amen, and hope
> they are well fed)

Wrapped in paradisal sea, I feel
the opposite of drowning.

Beginning again…
I would film myself eating the fruit,
and thus the exponential growth, and thus
the fucking, the contagion, and the
automated journey to the bottom.

Acknowledgements

I'd like to thank the magazines that published some of these poems: *The White Review*, *Poetry Review*, *HOTEL*, *Still Point*, and *Blackbox Manifold*.

I'd like to thank those who gave me support, creatively and emotionally, while writing this pamphlet:
Alex, Sam, Fraya, my mother, my father, George, Georgia, Chris, Chelsea, Martha, Kieran, The Garden Ward Girls, Maxwell, Theremin, Stylites, Morgana, and many more.

Final acknowledgements must go to God, Joelle, and Courtney Love.

Other titles by Out-Spoken Press